RICHARDSON

Find it!

On a car journey

Published by Richardson Publishing Group Limited.
www.richardsonpublishinggroup.com

10 9 8 7 6 5 4 3 2 1

© Richardson Publishing Group Ltd 2022.

Design by Junior London Ltd, junior.london. Illustration by Jonathan Mortimer.

ISBN 978-1-913602-22-2

Printed and bound by Bell & Bain Ltd, 303 Burnfield Road, Thornliebank, Glasgow G46 7UQ.

A catalogue record for this book is available from the British Library.

If you would like to comment on any aspect of this book, please contact us at:

E-mail: puzzles@richardsonpublishinggroup.com

🐦 Follow us on Twitter @puzzlesandgames
📷 instagram.com/richardsonpuzzlesandgames
f facebook.com/richardsonpuzzlesandgames

Contents

Introduction

Find it! books are designed to foster a love of learning and exploring the world through having fun.

Each of our books contain twenty-five things to find in the world around you, along with amazing facts and mind-bending puzzles.

Solutions to the puzzles can be found in the back of the book along with a place to make notes on your finds and a summary chart of the things to find. You can use the summary chart as an index to quickly locate your finds within the book or you can cut it out of the book and use it to find things on your travels!

Once you have found everything, there is a certificate at the very back of the book which you can ask a parent or guardian to complete and award to you!

For every 3 books completed, a parent or guardian can send us a message in order to receive a Find it! Super Spotter badge (T&Cs apply)! Simply fill in the form on our website at: richardsonpuzzlesandgames.com/superspotter

Happy finding!

Introduction

Tick this box when you have found the object. If you have a friend or sibling with you, why don't you set up a game to see who can find the most objects each?

Activity to complete!

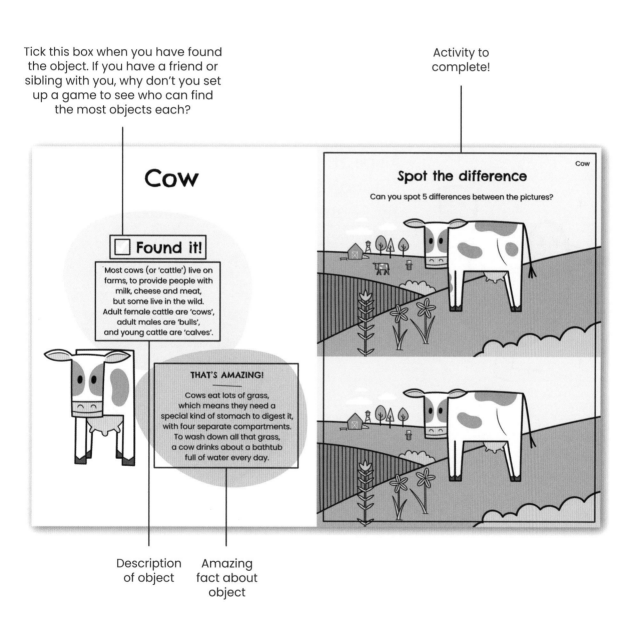

Cow

☐ **Found it!**

Most cows (or 'cattle') live on farms, to provide people with milk, cheese and meat, but some live in the wild. Adult female cattle are 'cows', adult males are 'bulls', and young cattle are 'calves'.

THAT'S AMAZING!

Cows eat lots of grass, which means they need a special kind of stomach to digest it, with four separate compartments. To wash down all that grass, a cow drinks about a bathtub full of water every day.

Cow

Spot the difference

Can you spot 5 differences between the pictures?

Description of object

Amazing fact about object

Bird

☑ Found it!

All birds have feathers and wings, though some don't use them to fly. There are many thousands of different kinds, from the tiny bee hummingbird, just 5 cm (a fraction under 2 in) long, to the enormous ostrich, which can be 2.75 m (nearly 9 ft) tall!

THAT'S AMAZING!

Birds are the descendants of a particular kind of dinosaur, which lived more than 65 million years ago.

Draw a picture

Draw a picture of the bird you find.

Cow

☑ Found it!

Most cows (or 'cattle') live on
farms, to provide people with
milk, cheese and meat,
but some live in the wild.
Adult female cattle are 'cows',
adult males are 'bulls',
and young cattle are 'calves'.

THAT'S AMAZING!

Cows eat lots of grass,
which means they need a
special kind of stomach to digest it,
with four separate compartments.
To wash down all that grass,
a cow drinks about a bathtub
full of water every day.

Spot the difference

Can you spot 5 differences between the pictures?

Horse

☑ Found it!

Before engines were invented, horses were an important form of transport. They pulled carriages, heavy loads and farm machinery. Today they're mostly kept as pets.

THAT'S AMAZING!

Horses can sleep standing up, and lock their legs to stop themselves from falling over.

Wordsearch

Look for the 10 words hidden in the wordsearch puzzle. The hidden words will run down and across. There are no words that run backwards or on a diagonal.

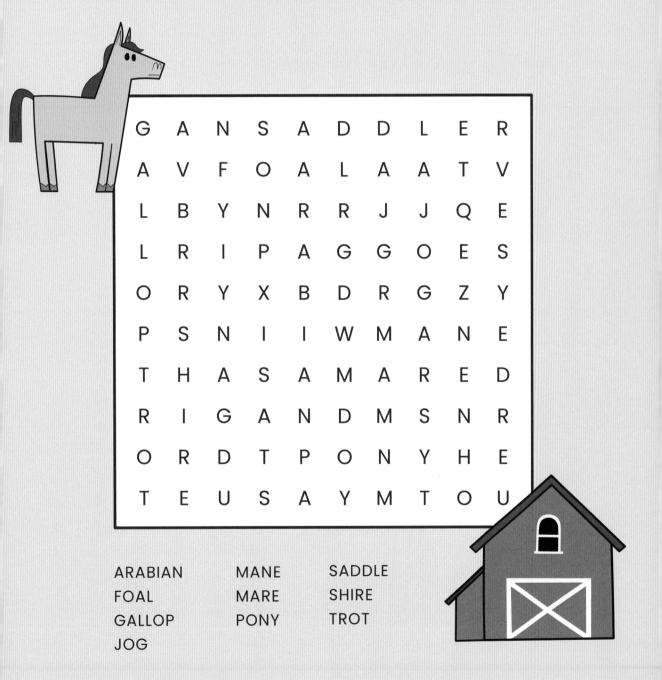

G	A	N	S	A	D	D	L	E	R
A	V	F	O	A	L	A	A	T	V
L	B	Y	N	R	R	J	J	Q	E
L	R	I	P	A	G	G	O	E	S
O	R	Y	X	B	D	R	G	Z	Y
P	S	N	I	I	W	M	A	N	E
T	H	A	S	A	M	A	R	E	D
R	I	G	A	N	D	M	S	N	R
O	R	D	T	P	O	N	Y	H	E
T	E	U	S	A	Y	M	T	O	U

ARABIAN   MANE   SADDLE
FOAL   MARE   SHIRE
GALLOP   PONY   TROT
JOG

Deer

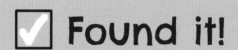 **Found it!**

There are more than 40 different kinds of deer, which live in the wild almost everywhere in the world.

THAT'S AMAZING!

Most male deer have antlers, but Chinese water deer have tusks – long, sharp upper teeth – instead.

Dot to dot

Connect the dots to uncover a picture, then fill in with pens or pencils.

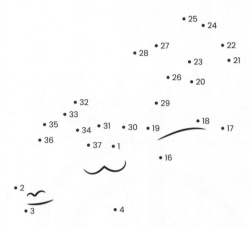

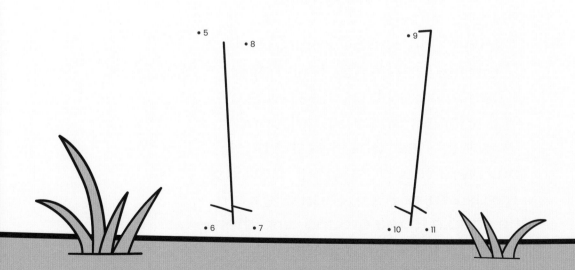

Bike

☑ Found it!

Bicycles are a great way to get around – you can travel quickly, without having to buy any fuel, and keep fit at the same time.

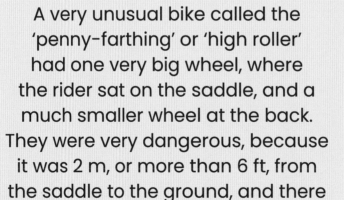

THAT'S AMAZING!

A very unusual bike called the 'penny-farthing' or 'high roller' had one very big wheel, where the rider sat on the saddle, and a much smaller wheel at the back. They were very dangerous, because it was 2 m, or more than 6 ft, from the saddle to the ground, and there were no brakes!

Spot the difference

Can you spot 5 differences between the pictures?

Motorbike

☑ Found it!

Motorcycles have two wheels,
like a bike, but are powered by
engines, so they can go much faster.
Riders have to wear a helmet and
special clothing to protect themselves.

THAT'S AMAZING!

The first motorcycles,
which were invented
over 150 years ago, were
powered by steam.

Maze

Take the road that leads back to the garage.

Police car

☑ Found it!

Police officers patrol the streets and speed to emergencies in police cars. Most police cars are marked so that everyone can easily identify them. Like ambulances, they use sirens and flashing lights in emergencies.

THAT'S AMAZING!

Some police cars are fitted with kennel seats for police dogs.

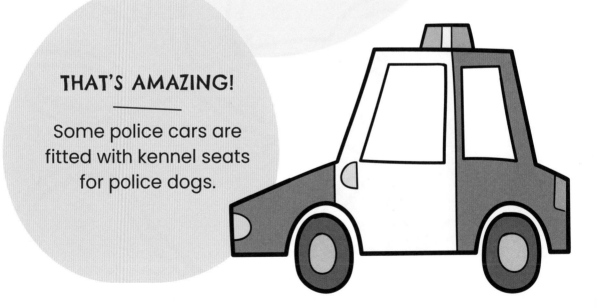

Telling the time

The policewoman takes 2 hours to get home from the police station after finishing her shift. If she leaves at the following times, when will she arrive home?

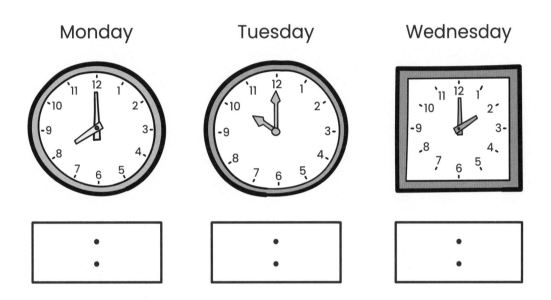

Monday

Tuesday

Wednesday

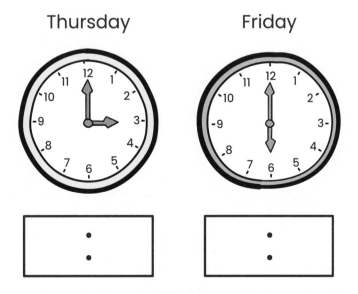

Thursday

Friday

Ambulance

☑ Found it!

If someone becomes very ill, or if there's an accident, an ambulance rushes to help. The driver and other ambulance staff are all trained for medical emergencies, so they can help the sick person, and take them to hospital if necessary.

THAT'S AMAZING!

Ambulances and police cars use a loud siren and flashing lights to alert other road users. The siren and lights vary in different parts of the world, and sometimes in different states within countries.

Complete the words

Complete the names of the places the ambulance has visited. The images next to the words are a clue. Cover them up if you would like to make the puzzle harder!

Z [ ] [ ]

P [ ] R K

F [ ] R M

S C H [ ] [ ] L

B [ ] [ ] C H

C H [ ] R C H

Campervan

☑ Found it!

Campervans mean that people can go on a camping holiday without having to put up a tent! The van drives around like an ordinary car or van but doubles up as a place to sleep.

THAT'S AMAZING!

Campervans might be fitted with a toilet, shower, bike rack, oven and grill, and solar panels to generate electricity.

Wordsearch

Look for the 10 words hidden in the wordsearch puzzle. The hidden words will run down and across. There are no words that run backwards or on a diagonal.

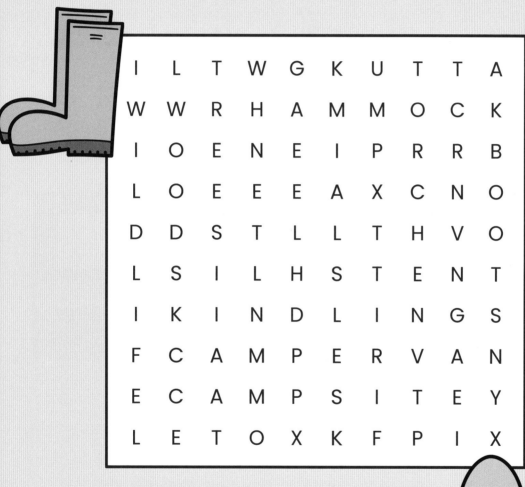

I	L	T	W	G	K	U	T	T	A
W	W	R	H	A	M	M	O	C	K
I	O	E	N	E	I	P	R	R	B
L	O	E	E	E	A	X	C	N	O
D	D	S	T	L	L	T	H	V	O
L	S	I	L	H	S	T	E	N	T
I	K	I	N	D	L	I	N	G	S
F	C	A	M	P	E	R	V	A	N
E	C	A	M	P	S	I	T	E	Y
L	E	T	O	X	K	F	P	I	X

BOOTS   KINDLING   TREES
CAMPERVAN   TENT   WILDLIFE
CAMPSITE   TORCH   WOODS
HAMMOCK

Bus

☑ Found it!

Buses carry lots of passengers in one vehicle – which is much better than having lots of separate cars on the road because it makes less pollution and uses less fuel.

THAT'S AMAZING!

The word 'bus' is short for 'omnibus', which means 'for everyone' in Latin, the language of the Ancient Romans.

Numbers

Subtract the numbers on the buses on the right from the numbers on the buses on the left. What are you left with? Use the number line if you need it.

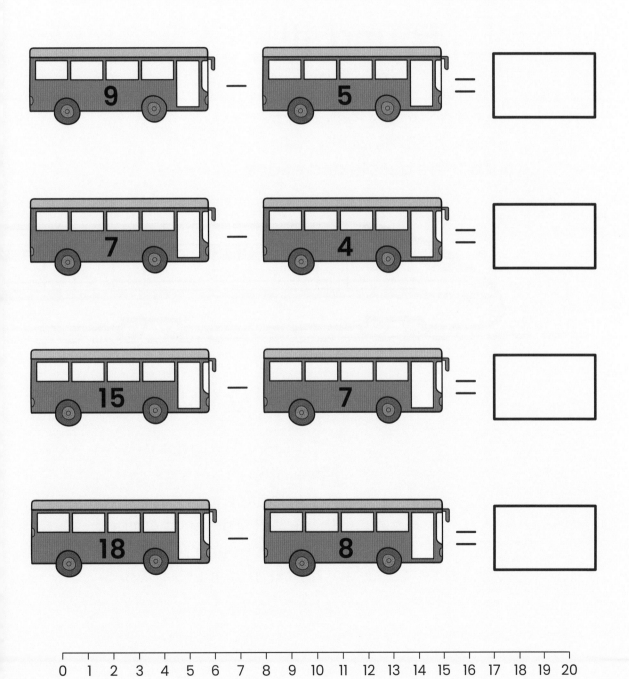

Train

☑ Found it!

Trains speed around the world on tracks faster than road vehicles can travel, transporting people and goods.

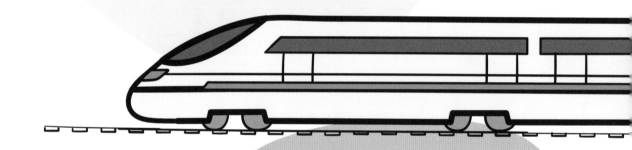

THAT'S AMAZING!

———

The world's fastest train glides along using magnets instead of tracks – it's the Shanghai Maglev in China, which has been recorded at 430 km/h, or 267 mph.

Telling the time

What times are the trains arriving?

Truck

 **Found it!**

Trucks carry heavy loads. There are different kinds: some are designed for transporting cars, fresh and frozen food can be carried in special refrigerated trucks, and concrete mixers have a spinning drum to mix concrete and a chute for pouring it out.

THAT'S AMAZING!

The world's biggest truck is a dump truck called BELAZ 75710. It can carry the weight of 75 African elephants!

Dot to dot

Connect the dots to uncover a picture,
then fill in with pens or pencils.

Excavator

☑ Found it!

Excavators work on construction sites and road works. They're mostly used for digging holes. Most use tracks instead of wheels to travel easily over bumpy ground.

THAT'S AMAZING!

The biggest excavators use an enormous wheel with lots of buckets on it. The Bagger 293 needs 5 people to operate it, and could dig the equivalent of 100 Olympic-sized swimming pools in just one day!

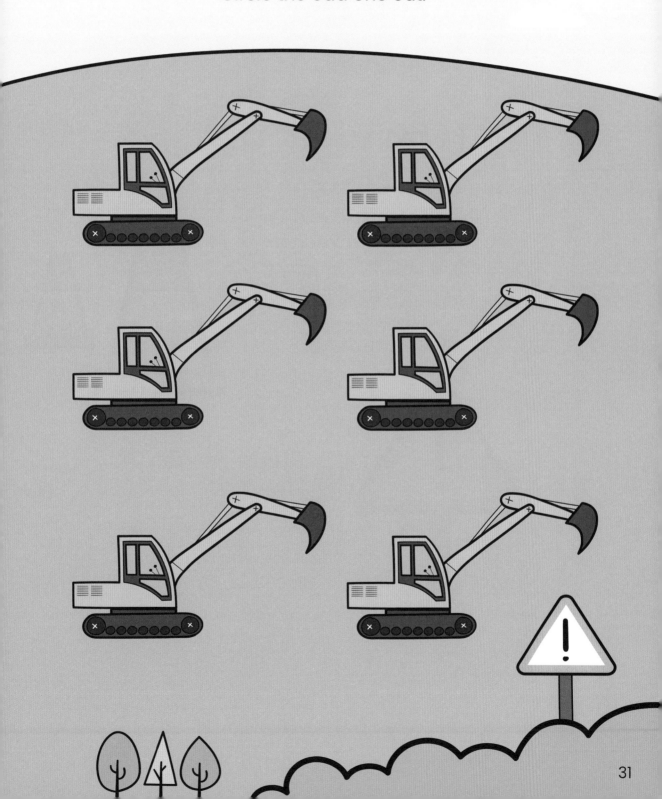

Spot the difference

Circle the odd one out.

Traffic cone

☑ Found it!

Traffic cones are used if vehicles need to avoid roadworks, or to travel in a different direction from usual. They're bright, sometimes with reflective surfaces, so drivers can see them easily.

THAT'S AMAZING!

The first traffic cones were made of concrete. Drivers had to make sure they didn't bump into them!

Numbers

Count how many cones with one stripe and how many cones with two stripes there are. If you add them together how many cones are there in total? Use the number line if you need it.

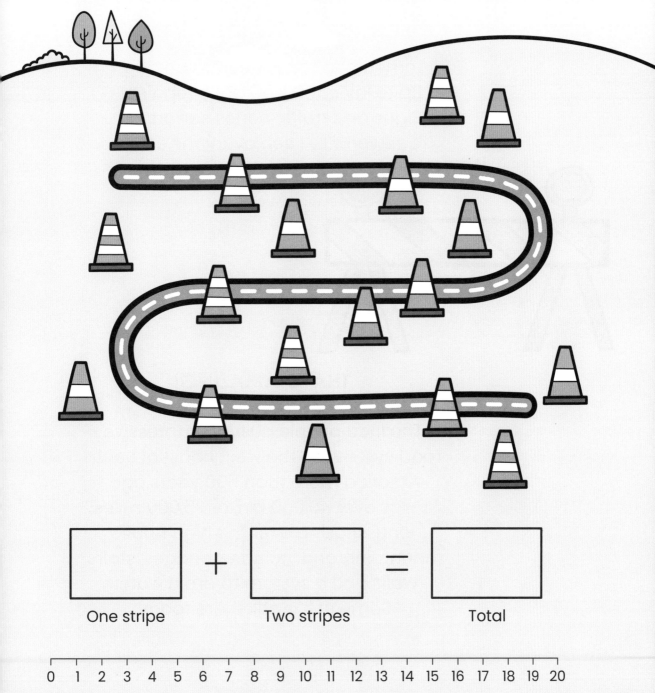

One stripe + Two stripes = Total

0 1 2 3 4 5 6 7 8 9 10 11 12 13 14 15 16 17 18 19 20

Roadwork

☑ Found it!

Sometimes roads need to be dug up to lay cables or make repairs. Signs and traffic cones surround roadworks to keep everyone safe.

THAT'S AMAZING!

The Inca people built an impressive road system on the west coast of South America more than 500 years ago. It was over 40,000 km, or 25,000 miles long, snaking over the high Andes mountains, and included bridges, stairs, walls and a system to drain water. Some of it is still there today.

Maze

Guide the worker to the hole in the ground.

Speed sign

☐ Found it!

30

Speed signs tell drivers the maximum speed they can go. It's important that vehicles travel slowly where there are lots of houses and shops so that people don't get hurt.

SPEED LIMIT 35

THAT'S AMAZING!

When cars were first invented there weren't any speed signs. In some countries, the law said someone had to walk in front of a car waving a flag to warn people that the vehicle was coming!

Numbers

Fill in the missing number for each sum.
Use the number line if you need it.

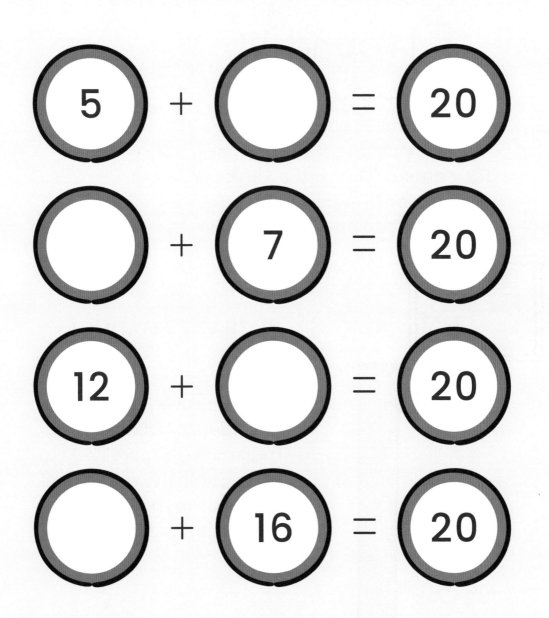

$5 + \boxed{} = 20$

$\boxed{} + 7 = 20$

$12 + \boxed{} = 20$

$\boxed{} + 16 = 20$

0 1 2 3 4 5 6 7 8 9 10 11 12 13 14 15 16 17 18 19 20

Speed camera

☑ Found it!

If a vehicle travels above the speed limit, a speed camera takes a photo as it drives past. The camera records the vehicle's registration number, so that the owner can be contacted.

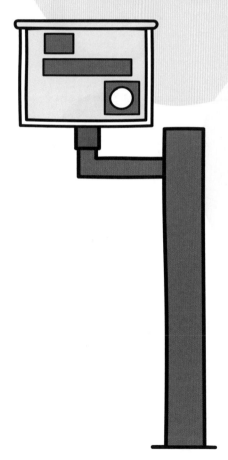

THAT'S AMAZING!

Speed cameras have been proved to reduce accidents, because they make drivers more likely to keep within the speed limit and drive more safely.

Dot to dot

Connect the dots to discover what vehicle has been caught by the camera, then fill in with pens or pencils.

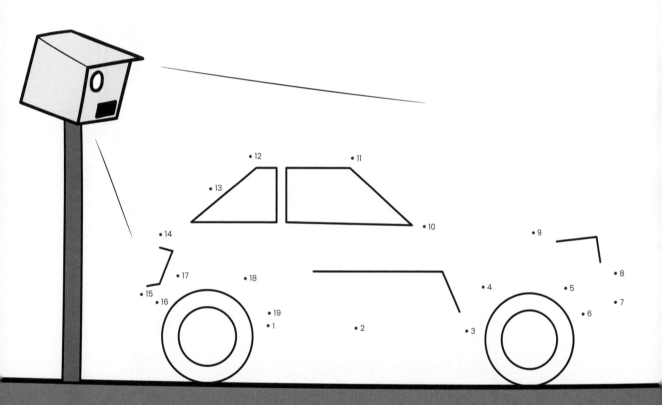

Traffic lights

☐ Found it!

Traffic lights are used to control traffic where two or more roads meet. They use a system of lights that's the same in all countries – red for stop, amber (or yellow) for get ready to stop or start, and green for go.

THAT'S AMAZING!

The latest traffic lights can have built-in cameras to detect vehicles and people so that they don't turn red for cars when there's no one crossing, or green when there are people waiting to cross but no cars.

Maze

Take the road that avoids the red lights!

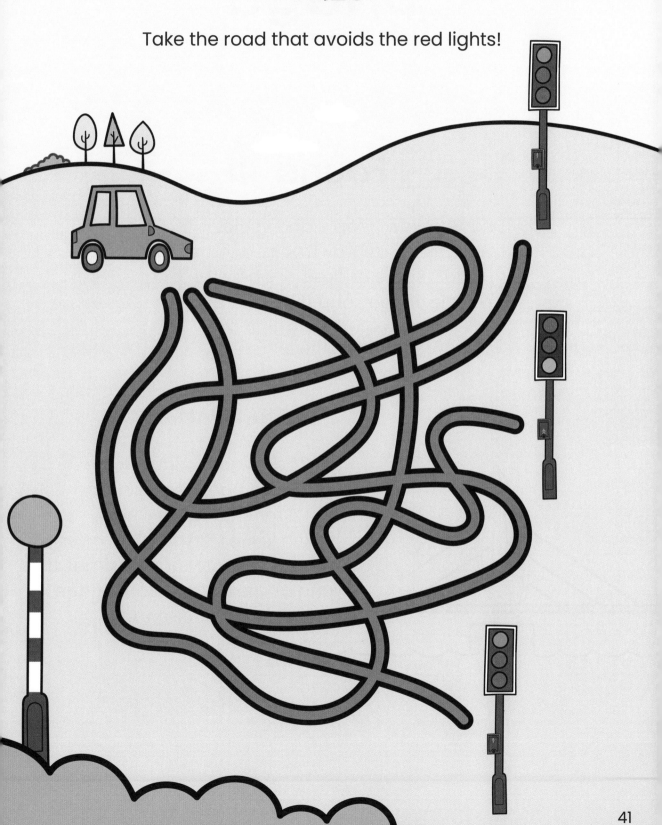

Bridge

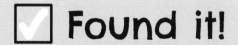

☑ Found it!

Bridges allow people and vehicles to cross rivers, railway tracks, or other roads. Some bridges are only for people on foot, and there are also bridges just for trains.

THAT'S AMAZING!

The longest bridge in the world is Danyang-Kunshan Grand Bridge in China, which is 164.8 km or 102.4 miles long. That's more than 60 times as long as the Golden Gate Bridge in San Francisco, USA.

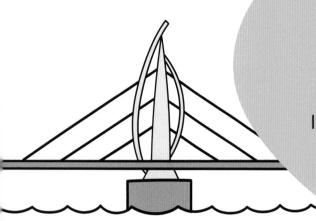

Complete the picture

Draw the other half of the bridge.

Service station

☑ Found it!

When drivers need a break from a busy road they can stop at a service station. They can fill up their vehicle with fuel, buy a drink and something to eat, and use the toilets.

THAT'S AMAZING!

When the first service stations opened in the UK in 1959, they were seen as glamorous destinations. Service station postcards were sold, so people could tell their friends they'd been somewhere exciting.

Matching pairs

Can you draw a line to link the yellow pump with
the yellow car and so on, without crossing the
lines or hitting the other pumps or cars?

Coffee shop

☑ Found it!

Coffee shops sell more than just coffee – tea, hot chocolate and other hot drinks, cola, juice, milk and milkshakes, and snacks.

THAT'S AMAZING!

Coffee is so popular that around the world people drink more than one thousand million (1,000,000,000) cups of it every single day.

Wordsearch

Look for the 10 words hidden in the wordsearch puzzle. The hidden words will run down and across. There are no words that run backwards or on a diagonal.

M	C	O	F	F	E	E	B	L	T
U	S	P	C	J	R	N	I	A	E
F	W	S	Q	S	A	E	S	C	A
F	S	A	N	D	W	I	C	H	Q
I	A	L	R	D	A	E	U	L	C
N	M	A	W	H	R	O	I	S	A
T	I	D	X	B	V	O	T	Z	K
U	L	P	P	A	S	T	R	Y	E
X	K	W	A	T	E	R	O	O	O
Q	M	J	H	U	K	G	B	H	K

BISCUIT   MUFFIN   SANDWICH
CAKE   PASTRY   TEA
COFFEE   SALAD   WATER
MILK

Hotel

☐ Found it!

People stay in hotels
when they go on holiday,
or if they have to travel
away from home.

THAT'S AMAZING!

Some hotels are very unusual.
You can stay in a cave in New
Mexico, USA; in an underwater
room in Zanzibar, Tanzania;
in hotels made of ice in the
Arctic; and a hotel made of
salt in Bolivia.

Spot the difference

Circle the odd one out.

Supermarket

☐ Found it!

Supermarkets sell all sorts of food, drink and other everyday items in one place.

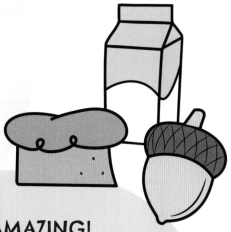

THAT'S AMAZING!

Before there were supermarkets, people went to lots of different stores – there were dry-goods stores, butchers', bakeries, and lots more. The first supermarkets set up shop more than 100 years ago, in the early 1900s.

Complete the words

Complete the names of the items on the shopping list. You will find clues on the facing page. Cover them up if you would like to make the puzzle harder!

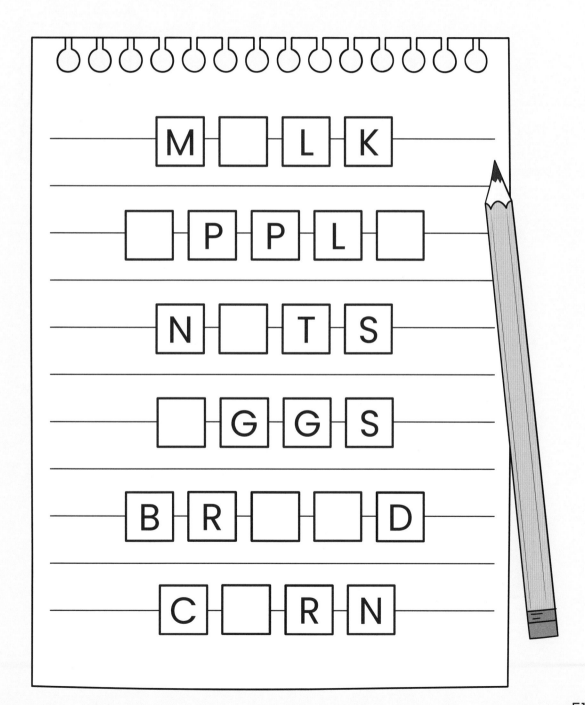

M ⬜ L K

⬜ P P L ⬜

N ⬜ T S

⬜ G G S

B R ⬜ ⬜ D

C ⬜ R N

Post office

☑ Found it!

Post offices deal with everyone's mail, from postcards to big parcels, and make sure it's delivered quickly and efficiently.

THAT'S AMAZING!

In the past, living things could be sent through the mail. In the early 1900s, a man called W. Reginald Bray from London, UK, successfully posted himself three times.

Maze

Guide the postman back to the post office.

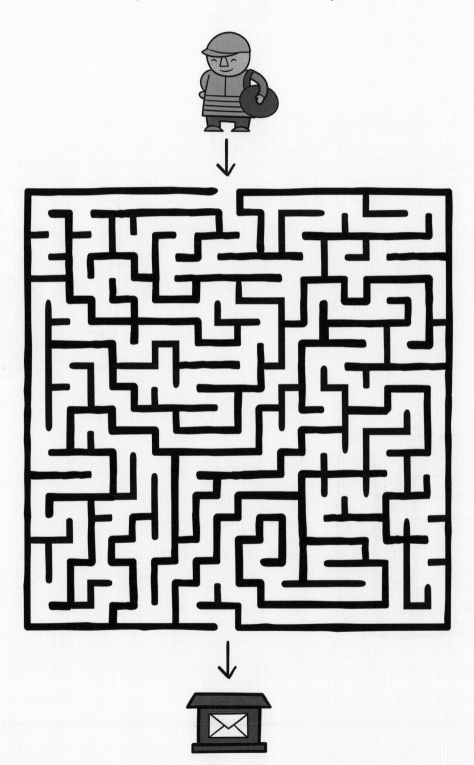

School

☑ Found it!

Most of the world's children go to school, where they learn mathematics, how to read and write, and about the world around them and its history.

THAT'S AMAZING!

Children often start school at the age of four. In Finland, children start school later than in any other country, at seven years old.

Telling the time

What time are each of the classes starting?

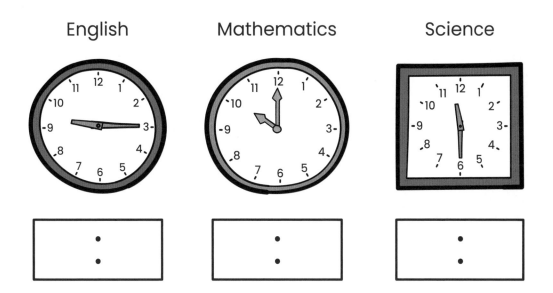

English

Mathematics

Science

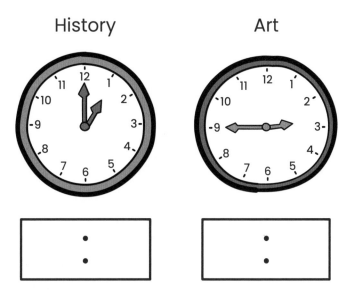

History

Art

Solutions

Page 09

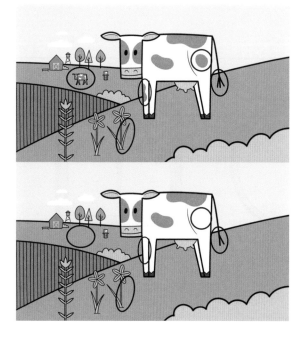

Page 11

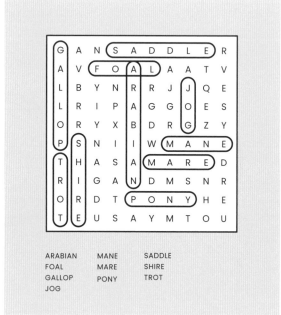

Page 13

Page 15

Solutions

Page 17

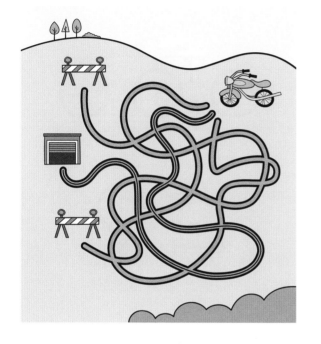

Page 19

Monday **10:00**

Tuesday **12:00**

Wednesday **4:00**

Thursday **5:00**

Friday **8:00**

Page 21

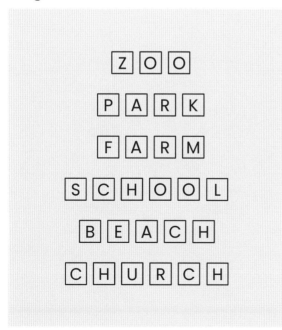

ZOO
PARK
FARM
SCHOOL
BEACH
CHURCH

Page 23

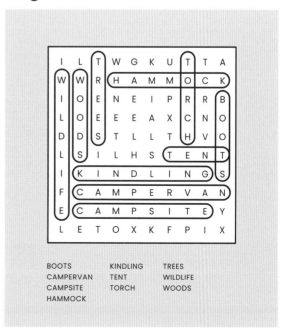

BOOTS
CAMPERVAN
CAMPSITE
HAMMOCK
KINDLING
TENT
TORCH
TREES
WILDLIFE
WOODS

Solutions

Page 25

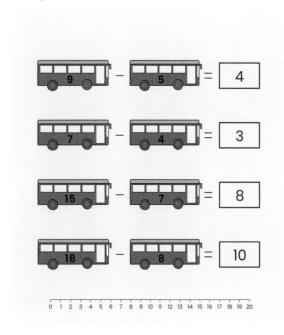

Page 27

Page 29

Page 31

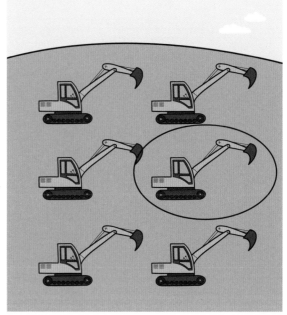

Solutions

Page 33

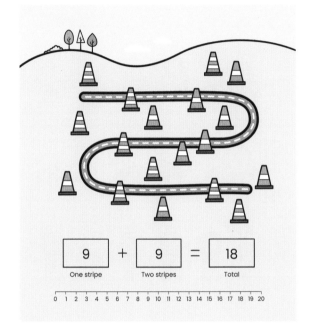

9	+	9	=	18
One stripe		Two stripes		Total

0 1 2 3 4 5 6 7 8 9 10 11 12 13 14 15 16 17 18 19 20

Page 35

Page 37

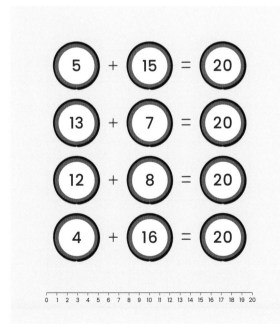

5 + 15 = 20

13 + 7 = 20

12 + 8 = 20

4 + 16 = 20

0 1 2 3 4 5 6 7 8 9 10 11 12 13 14 15 16 17 18 19 20

Page 39

Solutions

Page 41

Page 45

Page 47

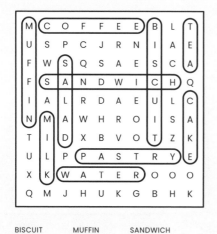

M	C	O	F	F	E	E	B	L	T

BISCUIT   MUFFIN   SANDWICH
CAKE   PASTRY   TEA
COFFEE   SALAD   WATER
MILK

Page 49

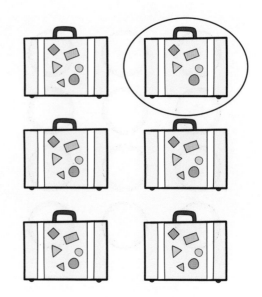

Solutions

Page 51

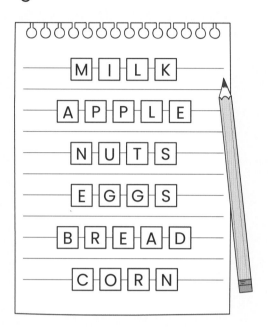

M	I	L	K

A	P	P	L	E

N	U	T	S

E	G	G	S

B	R	E	A	D

C	O	R	N

Page 53

Page 55

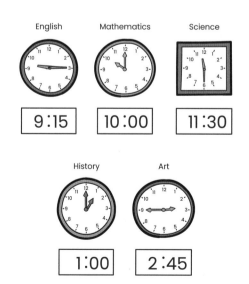

English
9:15

Mathematics
10:00

Science
11:30

History
1:00

Art
2:45

Notes on my finds

_____

_____

_____

_____

_____

_____

_____

_____

_____

_____

_____

_____

_____

_____

Chart of my finds

Finds by:

....

Use this chart as an index to quickly locate your finds within the book, or you can cut it out of the book and use it to find things on your travels. An adult can also use this page to confirm your finds!

Ambulance		p.20	Police car		p.18
Bike		p.14	Post office		p.52
Bird		p.06	Roadwork		p.34
Bridge		p.42	Service station		p.44
Bus		p.24	School		p.54
Campervan		p.22	Speed camera		p.38
Coffee shop		p.46	Speed sign		p.36
Cow		p.08	Supermarket		p.50
Deer		p.12	Traffic cone		p.32
Excavator		p.30	Traffic lights		p.40
Horse		p.10	Train		p.26
Hotel		p.48	Truck		p.28
Motorbike		p.16			

Find it!

Certificate

This certificate is awarded to:

....

For completing:

Find it! On a car journey

....

Date: ....